Through The Eyes of A Queen
Receiving While Bleeding

Latolya Cohen

Published by Japurjay Publishing

Copyright © 2015 Latolya Cohen

All rights reserved.

ISBN-13: 978-0-578-12144-4
ISBN 10: 0578121441

Dedication

Now that I have been a pastor's wife for a while, I can plainly see why so many pastors' wives are depressed, are in a backslidden state, or have even walked out on God totally. Because of my experiences, I can feel your pain and my heart goes out to each of you. I read Dr. Jerry A Grillo, Jr.'s book, " 7 Strategic Prayers to Pray over Your Pastor, " and was encouraged by it but heart broken by the statistics he noted about pastors' marriages and their wives. Dr. Grillo, Jr., founder of The Favor Center Fellowship, Hickory, North Carolina, states in his book that 50 percent of pastors' marriages will end up in divorce, over 50 percent of pastors' wives feel that their husbands' entrance into the ministry was the most destructive decision ever made concerning their family, 80 percent of pastors' wives feel unappreciated by the congregation, and 80 percent of pastors' wives feel pressured to be someone they are not and do things they are not called to do in the church.

Again, I say shocking, but true. So many people look at the first lady's position as one in the spotlight but they don't understand the process, the pain, the expectations of people and the fiery trials associated with being chosen for the position. Yes, we go through much behind the curtains. There are so many constant battles. The statistics cited above show just how much pressure first ladies are under. Many of us choose to walk away from our marriages and our assignments because we feel we can't handle them. And many of us have even turned our backs on God and refused to return to church because of cruel church folk. I wrote this book from the depths of my heart to your hearts to share my testimony and encourage you, first ladies, to hang on in there and don't give up. There is a breakthrough with your name on it. God does see your tears, your pain, and He hears your prayers as you pray His Word. Remember, He watches over His word to perform it. He's coming through for you in a great way. I Love You, Chosen Ladies. And remember, YOU WERE ANOINTED FOR THIS.

Contents

Acknowledgements		Pg# vii
1	God Chose You	Pg# 1
2	Conditioned for the process	Pg# 13
3	The trial	Pg# 19
4	The Season of dishonor	Pg# 24
5	Competition with the Church	Pg# 30
6	Becoming A Prayer Warrior	Pg# 36
7	Receiving While Bleeding	Pg# 40
8	Walking in Forgiveness	Pg# 48
9	The Turnaround	Pg# 53
About the Author		Pg# 59

Acknowledgements

First, I would like to thank my heavenly Father above for making all things possible. There is no me without Him, and I cannot produce anything productive outside of Him. I really thank Him for speaking to my spirit throughout my assignment and developing in me a heart for others who have received this assignment, too. My prayer is that this book will reach them. I'm grateful through it all because He could have chosen someone else. So, I count it a privilege to be employed by Him.

Second, I would like to thank my parents, Buford Royal, Jr. and Mary Royal, for being the vehicle that God could use to get me here on earth to be used by Him. I thank you for your constant love and support even when you didn't understand my choices or decisions; for your constant prayers for the will of God to be manifested in my life and your belief that He would take care of me in your absence. There were times I saw puzzled looks on your faces and, believe me, I was just as puzzled as you were, but I knew I had a CHARGE TO KEEP AND A GOD TO GLORIFY. It took you letting go of your little Keyon Royal, as you birth me, so that God could mature and make His Latolya Cohen who He created her to become. Oh, how I love you guys; you are awesome parents I must say. I honor you, and I pray that God gives you that Mal. 3:10 blessing.... "that there shall not be room enough to receive it."

Third, I am eternally grateful to and for my wonderful husband, Dr. L.E. Cohen. My God! An anointed vessel of God, for real. I really thank you and appreciate you for your obedience even when you didn't understand. God used you in such a phenomenal way to break, process, make, mold, and birth me. Without this arrangement by God, I would not have the experiences nor the words to say to those for whom this book is intended. I honor, love, and really respect you, sweetie, in a way beyond my understanding. It's a God-birth love and only through Him was it created. Thanks for being my teammate as we suffered together. Guess what? We also shall reign together. I feel a refreshing and newness in the atmosphere in such a way that it brings joy from within when I look upon your face.

Next, I would like to thank all of the men and women of God who spoke the Word of the Lord to me concerning this book. I don't want to get into any trouble naming names so I won't start just in case I forget one. You know who you are. Thanks to all of you.

From a teenager to now, Katrisha Williams has been a friend who always believed in me, even on those days that I couldn't believe for myself. She encouraged and coached me, was very real with spiritual counsel when I needed truth, and extremely supportive of me in my assignment from my Heavenly Father.

Last, I personally want to thank my God-given friend in the Lord, Minister Geraldine Harris. You have shown yourself to be a wonderful and trustworthy confidante — the type of woman of God who many first ladies need in their lives. Our friendship was fought, challenged, and questioned but God showed me just why He chose you. He knew that I would have to go through the most shameful time in my life and need your wisdom and support to get through it. You stayed right there, praying me through, believing in me even when I got weak at times, and covering me when I was battling in my mind. The sacrifices that you made to make sure that I was OK never went unnoticed. There were times when you sacrificed spending time with your wonderful husband, Minister Eric Harris, to keep me focused on God. And I love you dearly for that. May God bless each of you a hundredfold for your labor of love and the countless hours that you remained faithful to Him in the assignment to help not only me but the Prophet as well. To minister to us and to cover us the way that He showed you. Thanks, you guys. You are the Best.

To the pasture of sheep that we shepherd at In His Presence Cathedral Of Praise, Tallahassee, Florida, blessings upon each of you. I love you guys with all of my heart. Continue to push the Vision of the House as we continue to grow, in the name of Jesus.

1

God Chose You

You didn't choose me, I chose you. I appointed you to go and produce lasting fruit, so that the Father will give you whatever you ask for, using my name.

—JOHN 15:15, NLT 2ND EDITION

As I began to meditate on this passage of scripture, I thought back on my life as I knew it. I was minding my own business and thought I had the course of my life well figured out. To my surprise when I began to get very serious about God -- searching His Word for answers, trying to be obedient to His Word, living a low key life -- I gave Him a YES. And that's when my life was turned upside down. Luke 9:24-25, NLT, says, *"If you try to hang on to your life you will lose it. But if you give up your life for my sake you will save it. And what do you benefit if you gain the whole world but are yourself lost and destroyed?"* I was a bona fide Baptist girl. I didn't have a clue what giving up my life meant while not knowing where I would end up. I had heard it said on numerous occasions that God chooses people, but I didn't fully understand that being chosen meant He had a specific assignment for you in the earth for His Purpose.

God has a way of aligning you beyond what you can comprehend. He is so strategic in the assignment He designs for His chosen. You can be on the east coast, but God needs you on the west coast. He will strategically arrange and rearrange things in your life to create a window of opportunity, for a way of escape to get you in place. He does not care whose feelings get hurt. He needs for His will to be done in the earth by the vessel chosen for the task.

For example, I was part owner of a beauty salon in my hometown in Georgia when He came to me and said, "GO and do My will." My response was, yes, God, I will Go, not knowing that He had a top of the line, upscale salon with my name on it waiting for me in my predestined place. I was making good money, had clients who loved me, and the rent on the building was so affordable. What's more, this place was the result of me stepping out on faith to become an entrepreneur. The call put my natural mind in a quandary. Do I lose my life to save it or gain the whole wide world and lose my soul trying to consume wealth and gain? Because I knew that God was saying "follow Me and trust Me," I certainly didn't want to lose out, so I chose to follow Him and let go of the salon. I didn't have a clue how He was going to provide but just believed that wherever He guided me, He also would provide for me.

Not only did He challenge me in my career but also in my ministry affiliation. Remembering back, there was such a thirst in me for more of the Word of God that it seemed as though it burst up out of nowhere. I began to pray and ask Him to show me the place that He had ordained for me to get fed. Prov. 3:5-6, KJV says, *Trust in the Lord with all of thine heart; and lean not unto thine own understanding. In all thy ways acknowledge him, and he shall direct thy paths.*

Well, this is when I began to operate according to the Word. In times past, I did what I thought was best for me. For example, if all of my family were gathering together, then I would be there. Or, if my friend invited me to her ministry, I would go but sometimes would leave feeling just as empty as when I went. Now, however, I realize that coming into the place of alignment, my destiny, so that my life could be revealed depended on me being in the right place. Don't get me wrong, family churches are good but sometimes they can be a bit controlling. And if there is a calling on your life, sometimes it's your family who can't see past who you used to be or what they know about your past. Don't go jumping all over me for that! Some of you know that's true. (You can pick the book back up now and continue to read.) I sense somebody saying this girl has lost her mind talking about the family church. Cut that out! I love my family and from time to time will go back to visit, as the Spirit leads. But during that time in my life, it was imperative to separate.

I had a cousin who attended Wings of Faith International Ministries under Bishop Dreyfus C. Smith. It was a two-hour drive from my hometown to the church. After hearing her talk about how powerful the Word was and the atmosphere illuminated with the Spirit of God, I wanted to check it out. Lo and behold when I went, Lord, have mercy, I couldn't believe the teaching flowing from the man of God's mouth. God used him to break open the Word so plainly that even a child could understand it. After many visits, I felt in my spirit to become a part of the ministry.

The Word was bringing such a transformation to my life -- tearing down walls, plucking up roots, destroying the old mindset, and bringing about a new me. This was another stepping-out-on-faith move that I took on the path that God was leading me on. Anytime you make a conscious decision to do right, be right, and stay right, the enemy is on the prowl, strategizing to throw you off. When you are chosen for something, don't think the enemy is going to let you just walk into it. He knows how much of a threat you will be to his kingdom so he will do whatever and go to any length to try to destroy you. I vividly recall the morning that I read Dr. Mike Murdock's Morning Motivation that stated, "Avoid those who disrespect your chosen focus." He went on to say, "The only reason men fail is Broken Focus. Satan dreads your total concentration on God's Assignment in your life. When he wants to destroy you, he sends a person into your life. Delilah broke Samson's concentration. Broken focus made him a slave. Those who hear you should be the only ones near you." *Be not deceived: evil communications corrupt good manners.* I Cor. 15:33, KJV.

We don't really think about who we communicate with or how what they say can cause us to move in all sorts of directions. Nor do we really realize the negative impact of the conversations we have with ourselves. OK, don't get super saved on me now. You have conversations within your mind, too, that have you agreeing with those evil thoughts to follow your flesh. Everyone has them until they learn better. My maternal grandmother used to always say, when you learn better, you do better. So some of us have just learned to do better from the mistakes that made us wiser. OK, back to the story. I was just at Step One, allowing the Word to wash my mind from the past when I had a 1 Pet. 5:8, GW, experience. It says, *Keep your mind clear and be alert. Your opponent the devil is prowling around like a roaring lion as he looks for someone to devour.* My mind became my opponent because I thought I knew what I was doing. Paul said in Phil. 2:5, KJV, *Let this mind be in you, which was also in Christ Jesus.* Jesus had an obedient mindset to His Father. And when He says let, that means we have to allow His mind to be in us. He will not force us.

I was so excited about positive changes in my life that my flesh wanted now to be recognized, and I opened myself up for the set back. I looked for a friend because I felt lonely. Please hear me readers! You can avoid the mistake that I made. Simply take heed to the warning. I thought I could do God and do me at the same time. Needless to say, I was so wrong. Christians say, God understands. He knows me. Yes, He does know you. That's clearly why he says, *But seek ye first the kingdom of God, and his righteousness; and all these things shall be added unto to you.*" Matt. 6:33, KJV. I began seeking for me and not the kingdom, making a complete mess. It was not righteousness, but flesh. This was a disastrous plan from the pits of hell to draw me back and, for a moment, it did. It was designed to destroy me. It altered my time of being happy going to church, to spending my time doing me.

My life took a turn for the worse. I was driving home from my friend's house in the Chevy Trailblazer that God had blessed me with when I flipped it out in the middle of nowhere. It was pitch dark and there was no sound of cars at that time of night. It was smashed in all over except right over my head. The angels were on their assignment that night because my vehicle landed in a field just a couple of feet away from a deep pond but ended up on the side of the road. How did I walk away unscathed from this tragic accident? The only answer is my Father was watching over me to save me for what I had to do. My credit went down the hole for six months. I was in this relationship and running from the call. My money completely dried up. I was just getting by. The entrapment was so horrible that I wouldn't wish it on my worst enemy. I learned a valuable lesson from that incident. I had to go back to the same One I had left, my Father in Heaven, to get me out of it, in the name of Jesus. Some people would rather wallow in their mess. Oh, no, not me. The way out was calling me. For those who are reading this book right now and feeling that there's no way out, know that there is a way out for you as well. Please take that way. You never know when that opportunity will come again.

There were flyers posted announcing that a Prophet was going to be in town. Something began to turn inside of me as if my spirit was saying, 'You need to be there.' My friend was trying to do any and everything he could to make me feel bad about going, accusing me of men, picking unnecessary arguments and just plain showing his behind. Now that's just like the enemy; believe me, he knows when his time is just about up so he will do whatever to distract you from breaking free. But can somebody say, But God! I began to make arrangements to go to hear the Prophet anyway and, to my surprise, they came together.

Listen readers. God knows how to arrange things to come together to bring His plan forward when enough is enough by touching the hearts of people. On the first night of the revival, my mom drove my cousin and me there. The Prophet came right to my address (that means he began to speak, as the Spirit gave utterance, directly to my situation). He began to say, 'I see where there is a big snake around you. There is an assignment from the enemy to destroy you.' In hearing this I began to say, OK God, I need for you to come through for me right now. The detachment process began that night. I was now in a place where I needed the Jesus in me to be strong in my weakness to clean up the mess that I had made. My question to myself was, how am I going to get this man out of this house (a rental we shared together)? Moral standards were compromised in a great way. Shacking up, living as though I was right but all the time directly wrong in open rebellion. What I reaped was open shame. We really have to be careful about what we sow because we will reap it. I was sowing open rebellion to my God and, yes, the shame that I felt and that was displayed for everyone to see came as no surprise behind it. Two weeks later, the Prophet came back to town and he began to speak to me, 'The choice is in your hands.' I hadn't at that time made a clean get away but was making the necessary adjustments in other things. I began to talk to God for real now saying, now Father, I need to get it right immediately. Give me the strength to do what I need to do or You be the strength and make a way and I will follow You. I went home that night and an argument broke out about nothing really and the words " I want you out" came out of his mouth. I became angry when I reflected on the fact that getting out was not just about me. I also had two sons at the time. My thoughts were, I'm not going out like this. You're putting me and my kids out. I felt a rage burst open in me that was about to cause me to do something I would have deeply regretted. Then I was quickened in my spirit with a question, 'Didn't you ask me to make a way?' This was my way of escape. 1 Cor.10:13, GW states, *There isn't any temptation that you have experienced which is unusual for humans: God, who faithfully keeps his promises, will not allow you to be tempted beyond your power to resist. But when you are tempted, he will also give you the ability to endure the temptation as your way of escape.* I was tempted to retaliate for the sake of my kids. What did he care, they weren't his. I came to myself, got a couple of things, and went back to the place I had left, which was an apartment with my sister, until I could come back to get all of my things. That was the end of that.

Some people don't come out of things that easily. You sometimes have stalkers who will try to seek out your every move because you are not with them. It was by the grace of God that I did. This mistake made me understand how important it is, especially when you have kids, not to allow a man to move into your life so fast if he's not the one. Not only did I endanger myself but I put my kids in a confused atmosphere that I had to clean up. Situations like these can frustrate children and even cause them to be unstable in life, if that's all they see. I didn't want them to have to go through that again, so I straightened up.

After a while, I began searching for a new beginning for us. We needed a fresh start and new lease on life. One Saturday, I rode to a town about 45 minutes from my hometown to see what housing was available. I found an apartment complex that was open. The environment was nice and the rent half the price of what I was paying before. I took the application, returned home, and began to seek God further for a confirmation. The next week, flyers were going around about the Prophet coming to my hometown again. There were so many testimonies about him in my family and from the people in the town where he had prophesied before that I was afraid of him. He was known for his accuracy and electrifying spirit. When he opened his mouth, people knew answers and directions were going to flow through him from God. I walked in that night and the service was so awesome. And then he began to prophecy to me, 'I see boxes around you. There's getting ready to be a move in your life.' Then he paused and said, 'Actually there are going to be two moves in your life. The first move is for detachment, and the second move is to your destiny.' He proceeded to say, 'There are wolves God has to get you away from.' He was the very first Prophet to ever prophesy to me. Wow! I thought the drama was over with the relationship but there were still friends or people around me who I thought were genuine but the Spirit revealed what I was blinded to. Don't you just love that Jesus loves us so much that He does not allow things to stay hidden?

I went home and began to prepare for the first move but with questions in my mind about this second move. I wasn't questioning the Prophet, I was just in shock about the prophecy. God was moving rather quickly for me and I didn't have a clue what was going on or what was about to go on. When you are chosen, a lot of things don't make sense. He just wants to know that you trust Him. Our ways are not His ways, neither are our thoughts like His. Throughout the night, I dreamt that I was traveling with a man of God and he took me to meet a powerful woman of God who told me that I had fear in me that needed to come out. I had no idea what it meant. I told you I was afraid of the Prophet. And the idea or thought of having to be in a man of God's presence too long caused angst. The conversation in my mind went something like this: He sees all through me. I didn't play with God's anointed.

There was a continuation of the revival the next week. This time a man of God whom I'd never seen came to town along with the Prophet. This Apostle could see dry land through muddy water. This man of God laid those eagle eyes on me and began to prophecy, bringing confirmation to everything the Prophet had said. He even began unfolding the dream and began to speak as I walked toward him. He saw the powerful woman of God in the dream I had, called her out by name and saw her step into my body. He said, 'You are going to preach the Word. Yes, you are. And let me tell you this (he told the musicians to stop playing), you are a first lady. I was frozen in motion at that, because I knew there was a possibility of me preaching because it was in my bloodline. As a matter of fact, my deceased paternal grandmother, Pastor Eddie Mae Royal, was a mighty woman of God. And my deceased maternal grandmother, Bernice Atkins, was the church mother. Church was in me from birth, and I knew I would be in church doing something, but I didn't know to what extent. Back to the prophecy about me being a first lady. I remember saying to God, now you know that I'm afraid of this; you are going to really have to clean up my mouth and attitude for this one.

> I went off judging myself, in anticipation of what it would be like to be a first lady, as Jeremiah did in saying, 'Lord I am but a child, how do you expect me to do this?' Even though he was a youth, it was God who put his Words in his mouth and trained him for the task he had before him. You may have viewed your calling in the same way. If so, I encourage you to go to the One who chose you and say, Lord, you have chosen me to be a wife to your anointed, but I feel so unprepared. What must I do? And if you are one of the ones who feels as though 'I got this and will help him straighten these people out,' you have the wrong

attitude. When you are chosen for this task, it takes dying to one's self and taking the first approach, Lord, take me by my hand and walk with me. Remember that it was God who chose you, and He knows just what you have inside even when you don't. EVERYONE IS NOT HAPPY FOR YOU, but God is bragging on you. I must really stress that to you. There are many who are called but only a few chosen. You are very special when God chooses you. Please don't let Him down. Make your Father look good in this. In making Him look good, you sometimes may have to put a smile on your face even when you're hurting inside. For some this is hard because they feel as though they are living a lie. But I tell you this, through the smiles and continual battles in my mind and emotions, I know the Trinity walks with me. Did I question God's decision? Yes, I did, and I'm sure you do at times when things don't look the way they should. People will try to make you feel like you have to meet their requirements and expectations to be a first lady. I am happy to say, they weren't the one who called, purposed, or predestined you for this assignment. *For I know the thoughts that I think toward you, saith the Lord, thoughts of peace, and not of evil, to give you an expected end.* Jer. 29:11, KJV. I'm glad to know that He has the plan and not man. Were it left up to man, he would rip up the plan and put who he wanted in your place every time you didn't bow down, walk out when he thought you should, or break under the pressure of his expectations. I had to become just like Jesus. Can't no man take my life except I lay it down. Were there times I wanted to lay it down? Absolutely, but thanks be to the Holy Ghost who brings all things back to remembrance. He reminded me that it was not about me, and I couldn't view it as such. I had to ask for the heart, mind, and eyes of God because if He chose me for this assignment then He surely had equipped me to stand.

Before I formed you in the womb I knew you, before you were born I set you apart; I appointed you as a prophet to the nations. Jer. 1: 5, NIV. In looking at this scripture, God told Jeremiah, 'before I formed you, your destiny was with me, and I already knew what I was sending you to earth to do for me.' Think about that for a moment. Before we were in our mothers' wombs, God looked down on earth and had a conversation with Jesus and the Holy Spirit about us. It's almost as if He were saying, I have a need for some godly women to stand for me, to show my glory through themselves. Women who can take a licking and keep on ticking; pray my men of God through their battles, be their eyes when things are too close for them to see, and cover them at all cost. Now do you see your important need, women of God?

No, being a first lady is not easy. I had to really die to my flesh and must continue to die to it because of the vision God has set for the House, which depends on me to help birth it out. We sometimes get caught up in the many circumstances that make us want to say, forget covering him. He needs to cover himself because, right now, I'm the one who needs covering. I have said it and let's really be real, I have done it. It's through trial and error that we sometimes have to learn that we don't have a choice because He chose us. Unfortunately, this is like a secret life that often appears perfect outwardly but inwardly things are crumbling. It is difficult to get another first lady to be real with you about how difficult things can be. OK, back to the birthing. You may ask, how then do I birth this power to ward off the brutal attacks and continue to fulfill the charge I have and glorify God? The greatest breakthrough will come through your prayers, but others will come through the work of your hands. It amazes me how people look for the first lady to be the one who just sits with the big hats and looks pretty. Well, guess what? You can look pretty while warring in the Spirit. You can look pretty while singing in the Spirit, and you can definitely look pretty while being keen in the Spirit. He wouldn't have sent you here and put the charge on you if you were destined to fail. He knows you can do it; you have to know you can. Trust me, this took a breaking down in my mind for real just to get to this point. Remember, we die daily.

In the midst of it all, I began to say, Lord, I'm sorry that I complained about my calling because I did not fully understand it. And You know that I am still learning something new daily. One thing that I have come to realize is that God doesn't make mistakes, people do. Therefore, you should know that He has not mistaken your identity with someone else's. He knows the number of hairs upon your head and is too accurate to say, uh-oh. I meant to call sister so and so. In the beginning, I told a little of my background to let you know that I wasn't perfect, wasn't born with a silver spoon in my mouth as they say, nor was I praying to be the one. I prayed for the will of God and His will chose me.

For those of you who can identify with being chosen, and are battling with being chosen of God, know that He did not make a mistake. Yes, there will be trying times when you will have no clue how you will come out, but know that He will not leave you nor forsake you. He's just putting another anointing on you through the suffering, purifying, sanctifying, and polishing that will render you fit for His use.

LATOLYA COHEN

PRAYER

Father God, you are the Most High God in whom all things were made. You know my thoughts before I think them, my ways before I attempt them, and even my words before I speak them. Help me to embrace that it was You, Oh Lord, who chose me for this assignment and no one else. It was You who called me by name out of everyone else. Your Word says that You are able to keep that which is committed unto You. Father, I'm yours and I place everything about me into Your hands. I decree that I will keep my mind stayed on You so that You can keep me in perfect peace and peace shall be the ruler of my spirit. It is a must that I stay committed to the mission and married to the mandate because I have a charge to keep and a God to glorify. Get your glory, oh great King, out of the vessel You have chosen, as I continue to lift my eyes to the hills, from which cometh my help, knowing that all of my help comes from You. And I shall finish strong, in the name of Jesus I pray, Amen.

2

Conditioned for the process

*But in a great house there are not only vessels of gold and of silver,
but also of wood and of earth; and some to honour, and some to
dishonour. If a man therefore purge himself from these, he shall be a vessel
unto honour, sanctified, and meet for the master's use,
and prepared unto every good work.*

—2 Timothy 2:20-21, KJV

After moving into my place of destiny, God quickly began to take me through a very intense purification process. To purify means to cleanse or extract. To extract means to take a part from. (According to Webster's pocket new world dictionary.) When I think about purification, the process of refining gold immediately comes to mind. In order for gold to reach the purification intended, it must go through fire at the highest degree to burn off any impurities. Likewise, in order for us to reach the pureness in heart to be positioned the way He wants us to be, we must go through fiery trials. When I say fiery, it is an unexplainable fire that I didn't know that I would have to go through in God. For some reason, I thought when I said, yes, all of my troubles were over. But to my surprise that was not the case. The purpose of the purification was to break all of the soul ties from previous relationships, remove past ways, and strip the mindset that I had all of the answers and could figure out all things.

Let's start first with breaking the soul ties. What is a soul tie? The soul is the spiritual part of the person, the vital part. Webster's Dictionary further defines the soul as the principle of life, feeling, thought, and action in humans, regarded as a distinct entity separate from the body, deeply felt emotion. Tie means to bind in any way, fasten, or attach with a cord, string, or the like, drawn together and knotted, join or connect in any way, informal; to unite in marriage, to confine, restrict, and limit. Together they are a binding of feelings, a uniting, or a union. A banding together takes place. Therefore, anyone who I had been sexually involved with in previous relationships had emotional bonds intertwined in my spirit that had to be broken. We never think about the mystery that God created in the intertwining in marriage. If we did, we would have such a problem in our spirit when we go outside His marriage plan and have sex before marriage. Soul ties will have you acting just like the person you've connected with. When I really understood this, I felt so bad about sharing my body outside of marriage. That in itself made me repent. We really are destroyed for a lack of knowledge. My mind just went back to my foolish days. God knew how to show me my mistakes but in turn He gave me a message to help someone else. As first ladies, we really need to help this generation understand this concept, for real. I could not step into a man of God's life, bound to someone else, and think that I could be what he needed me to be. I had to go through this process.

A lot of times we look forward to just jumping into things or into relationships -- being happy about the person we're now dating, the conversations we share, and full of expectations for the future -- without asking ourselves, am I still wounded from my past? Am I still in love with the ex-friend? Or, am I looking for this relationship to cover up the emptiness stemming from loneliness? Sometimes God has to hold up things for a while to get us positioned the way that He needs us to be. At first I fought this process because of a lack of understanding, and who wouldn't? I said, God, I love you but I feel like you have tricked me. But after continuing to search the Word of God for understanding, and receiving confirmation from his men and women of God that what I was going through was necessary before I could get to where He was taking me, I had to let go of all possibilities of returning to my hometown. I then had to embrace the assignment and humble down in order for God to flow in me the way He needed to, that I may receive what He purposed for me. As a matter of fact, I remember receiving a word from a woman of God telling me that as soon as I let go of Georgia, the process would begin. I could tell when I had finally released my past because immediately, all hell broke out for me. I had to isolate from people, disconnect from communicating with my family, and avoid dealing with my future husband. Now imagine being in a place where there's no family or friends, and it's just you and God for the first time in your life? Honestly, I didn't know how to explain this to my parents. They were so worried and all I could tell them was that I was in the Hands of the Lord. Did they understand? Certainly not. But I thank my Jesus for comforting them in the words only I knew to say. My mother said to me once, baby, why don't you just come visit us and stay a little while. I responded to her, mom, you know that I love you but when it comes to what I have to answer to God for, this is where I separate the love. I have a charge to keep and a God to glorify. You may not understand now but through time you will see why all things had to be. With tears in her eyes, she hugged me and said, baby, be obedient to God because, in the end, you do have to answer to Him, and not to me. I will just continue to pray for you. I wanted to say, mom, I'm catching so much hell. It's not what I thought. I am in so much pain from letting go and letting God do what He has to so that I can be a vessel of honor, meet for His use. I hugged her so tightly and with humility again said, while holding back the tears, please, mom, pray that the will of God be manifest in my life, and it shall be.

    I called this place the land of the unknown because I had no clue what God was up to. He showed me the end but the middle was unfolding daily. He has a way of getting you to fall in love with Him so deeply that you just say, whatever You need me to do Lord, I will trust You. I had to face my fears, deal with my past attitude, and learn how to love me, although I thought I did only to find out that I really didn't know me. This was the secret place. I was flip with my mouth. Whatever came up came out. That practice now had to be adjusted. I had to speak with wisdom and to think about what I was getting ready to say before I said it. This was one of the dishonorable things that the lead-in scripture references. Words are not just words; they are spirit that brings life or kills. **Death and life** *are in the power of the tongue:* **and** *they that love it shall eat the fruit thereof.* Prov. 18:21, KJV. My words were my defense mechanism. If you hurt me, I had no problem telling you off. Whatever I thought needed saying to let you know the intensity of my hurt, I verbalized it. Ladies, know that this most definitely is something that I had to allow God to work on. He showed me how to speak what I needed to speak in the spirit and at the right time. You can say the right thing but at the wrong time and cause disaster in your home and relationship. Timing is so important; I can't stress that enough.

When you haven't gotten the OK in the Spirit realm that the timing and atmosphere are right to proceed in a conversation, to approach something that you are not comfortable with, or even share something that you see could be harmful to your man of God, your input sometimes will be rejected. And you will be looked upon as the "nagging" wife. This is where God taught me, In all thy ways **acknowledge** him, and he shall direct thy paths. Prov. 3:6, KJV. I can remember riding in the truck with my husband, fiancé at the time, along with our guest when he began yelling and screaming and really embarrassing me. I couldn't take it, so I began to yell back and threw a temper-tantrum about what he had said. To look back at that moment now, I see how immature I was. The guest came up to me later and said, anytime you may be upset about something, or you guys disagree on something, try not to debate it in front of people. I felt so small that I humbled down and said, you are right, and I won't do that again. Lesson learned. Did it happen again? Most certainly, but I had matured in that matter by then.

God really used my husband-to-be to break that mindset off of me. Did I think that it was fair? No, I didn't, but I appreciated who God used because had it been anyone else, I know I probably wouldn't have accepted it. Ladies, God will use our spouses to make us. You will say, oh, this is not fair. It seems as if You let them get away with so much God. But God says, *For my* **thoughts** *are not your* **thoughts**, *neither are your ways my ways, saith the LORD.* Isa. 55:8, KJV. If He chooses to think, OK I'm going to use her mate or sister so and so to get her where I need her to be, He's God and He has every right to and really there's nothing you can do about it but submit to His plan. Again, it took a minute for me to wrap my mind around this one.

Now, becoming conditioned to the pattern of this process was taking root as understanding increased. I used to run if things didn't look right or act right and that had to be broken or purged out of me, too. The hardest thing, I thought, was to be trained to stand, stick and stay where God had placed me no matter what it looked like. Why was this hard, you may ask? I was not married at the time, just being processed as Esther to be with the King. To be made to go through pain to be something that I was called to, just did not make sense. Back to where I mentioned that my mindset had to die, here is where it really had to die. Men of God are so anointed, powerful and prestigious. A lot of women find that attractive but don't understand the strength that being a first lady requires. Now that I look back, I really thank God for conditioning me before I had to reign because it was there that He showed me the strength I didn't know existed in me. He knows how much we can handle, and the strength each woman of God needs for the man of God He has for her. What I needed may not be what you need, because everybody is not the same. You will have to have the strength to carry your man of God in prayer during his time of weakness and your time of feeling left out. Wow! Was this a learning experience! It was in the conditioning that God instilled the anointing in me to Stand! The Spirit of God has to anoint you for the position and included in the position is the ability to Stand.

In your conditioning process, you may be challenged to stand and believe when it seems all odds are against you. There will always be somebody who looks as good as you do, still stand! Is as anointed as you are, still stand! Thinks they can do it better than you, still stand! Even try to compete with you, still stand!

PRAYER

Lord, I thank You for conditioning me for the process. Only You know what I need to be able to do what You've called me to do. I trust You in every plan that You have for my life. Jer. 29:11 says *that you know the plans that You have concerning me, thoughts of good and not of evil, and that You have an expected end for my life.* I embrace Your plan with my whole heart and only believe that it is working for my good. As You continue to unveil the things You have prepared for me, I will trust You and acknowledge You in all of my ways that I may not sway to the right nor to the left but to be careful to do all that You command because I love You. Thank You for causing me to examine myself and consider my ways -- letting go of what I could that You may deliver me from what I couldn't. In Jesus' name I pray, Amen.

3

The trial

Beloved, think it not strange concerning the fiery trial which is to try you, as though some strange thing happened unto you: 13) But rejoice, inasmuch as ye are partakers of Christ's sufferings; that, when his glory shall be revealed, ye may be glad also with exceeding joy. 14) If ye be reproached for the name of Christ, happy are ye; for the spirit of glory and of God resteth upon you: on their part he is evil spoken of, but on your part he is glorified.

—1 Peter 4:12-14, KJV

When I think about the word trial, the courtroom setting quickly comes to mind. Trial means, even to try, to prove or test. Being brought before a court to confirm or acquit a charge of wrongdoing (from The Student Bible Dictionary). The event in which God puts your faith on trial to prove your love will most certainly not be understood by men. The suffering will seem strange to you and just outright disturbing to others. No one knows the conversation that you and God had concerning the instructions given to you to take the test. Which is why v14 of the above scripture says *on their part he is evil spoken of, on your part he is glorified.* How is He evil spoken of? Many will stand back and judge you and your situation, say that you are crazy and that what you are doing is not God. You know what you have to do and doing it is glorifying your Father.

People will try to talk you out of what seems foolish to them but it's what God is using to confound the wise. It may come off as a concern, and you may have some that genuinely do care, but they just don't understand because the wisdom of God confuses the mind of the intelligent. Worldly wisdom is not godly wisdom so be very careful when idle chatter comes to you. If you allow talk to penetrate through you ear gate and cloud the understanding that you and God have, it may cause you to take your eyes off Him and instead start looking and meditating on the trial, causing you to lose focus.

While being on trial, it seems as though your life is an open book. Everybody's reading it, drawing their own conclusions. And you just want it to stop. In the midst of it all, He is birthing fruit of the spirit in you. The fruit of the spirit is the character of God. The trial is working for your good. Not only are you suffering to birth an anointing but now when they see you they see God. The suffering is not as a robber or thief but is for the glory of God to be revealed.

During my trial, I had to learn how to let God fight my battles, to trust in Him with all that was in me, and stand still to see His salvation. It was not easy because to hold your peace when you know you are right can be challenging. But hold your peace you must so that you don't ruin your testimony. No, I didn't get it right all of the time; yes, I did verbalize some things but then it seemed as though God started the time over or added more time on the clock. If I didn't get the understanding of the conditioning process, I knew that I had really flunked this one big time. I thank Him for being a God of another chance and having patience with me.

Let's talk a little about some of the trials that first ladies face. Church folk can be a trip. You wonder why they have the most pleasant looks but can be so ruthless and mean at times. In the beginning of this book, I mentioned that the statistics from Dr. Grillo Jr. showed that 80 percent of pastors' wives feel unappreciated by the congregation. This can even spill over into the home. You have to have a strong bond with your spouse and God has to be the glue that holds you all together, because when there is a sense of weakness in the marriage, the devil gets busy using the church folk. For so long, we have chosen not to discuss the known facts with our men of God. We just sit back and let the enemy run wild in our homes, marriages, and churches. But I decree and declare that this madness will come to an end as we stand up with the Spirit of God and take our rightful places. Some church folk will even try you just to see your reaction. You pray, cover, support and give your man of God the unconditional love that God requires you to give but still somehow it's not enough. To be righteous comes with a price of selflessness. Sometimes you want to say, God, let me close the book on this one and please turn your head because I GOT THIS! Then He comes to you and says, DO YOU TRUST ME? I don't know about you but at times that's the last thing I want to hear when my womanhood and assignment are being challenged. I was like, yes, Lord, but don't you see what's going on? Are you sure you don't need my help? I had to go through the public shame and humiliation that made me, at times, wonder and ask God, Is it worth it? Being quickened by the Spirit, I had to come back to myself and remember that the suffering was not for me even though I felt it. It was for someone else. He reminded me of how pleased He was when Jesus bore the cross, despising the shame, standing for what He was sent to do and carrying out the assignment regardless of how painful it was. In this trusted position, yes, you will have to carry a cross in front of many and sometimes even hang on it. There are sabotages that are concealed for a season until you mature and have the grace to handle Him showing you the underlying truth of what is going on.

    Let's define sabotage? Sabotage (Dictionary.com) is any underhand interference with production, work, etc., any undermining of a cause... Does this happen in ministry? Yes, it does. One reason pastors' wives feel unappreciated is their ideas are devalued by church folk and their spouses, resulting in a loss of respect. For example, when heading up different ministries to try to bring unity, opposing ideas may arise that conflict with or even contradict the vision God has given to the pastor's wife. If she proceeds with her ideas and their ideas are not used or are tabled, they sometimes take offense and choose not to be involved. Furthermore, they drop seeds of discord to others and withdraw their support. This continues to spread and before you know it, the assignment given by the pastor becomes a struggle -- people won't get on board and you are viewed as unqualified to help lead the flock. Your credibility is shot and everything you try to do, someone feels as though they can do it better. Now here you are saying, in spite of all of the effort I put forth to enhance and help the ministry and the support and love I gave out to so many, I am left to face feeling unappreciated. It just does not seem fair. God will use even that to cultivate the unconditional love in you by telling you to still love, still support, and still encourage in spite of how you feel. Did you say, Why should I? I'm glad you asked that question. Fiery Trials, the hot stuff that hurts so badly, can bring forth a new you if you embrace them. After my feelings were hurt bad so many times, I became numb to the hurt, unaware that deliverance was taking place. Looking back, I now realize that all of the hurt was necessary to bring healing to my emotions. Emotions can't be a ruling force or driving force in ministry no matter what position you are in. Especially being a pastor's wife, if emotions are displayed, many will view you as being weak and unable to handle anything. They will not follow you to something as simple as a dog fight because they feel you are not secure and confident. Prov. 24:10, KJV, says, *If thou faint in the day of adversity, thou strength is small.* Strength is being made in you when you continue to stand through heart breaks, disappointments, rejections, feelings of not being appreciated, sabotages, public shame, and embarrassment. It's all a part of you learning your role as God teaches and makes you through the trials.

PRAYER

Lord, You are my God in Heaven who knows what is best for me. You know how and what to use to develop me for I am Your workmanship. You called me from my mother's womb to be a representation of your kingdom here on earth. From the birth until You ushered me into my predestined place, I acquired some things that would not bring you honor. I lay down my will, my way and my understanding that You may work those things out of me that Your name may get the glory out of my life. I realize that though this may cause suffering in which I gladly partake of with Christ, that when Your glory shall be revealed, I may be glad also with exceeding joy. I will greatly rejoice in this season of trials knowing that the trying of my faith is working patience to make me complete and lacking nothing. In Jesus' name I pray, Amen.

4

The Season of dishonor

Instead of shame and dishonor, you will enjoy a double share of honor. You will possess a double portion of prosperity in your land, and everlasting joy will be yours.

—Isaiah 61:7 NLT

Along with the tests and trials that seem to be prevalent in every area of your life, you will also encounter a season of dishonor. To dishonor means to lose honor for or respect for, disgraced, shamed or a cause of shame, and to insult (Dictionary.com). The length of the season depends totally on God. In the midst of it, He develops you and causes you to realize and know who you are. Not everyone feels the need to respect wives, even pastors' wives. But you have to know that you are the one even when you are not treated like the one.

From childhood, I remember everyone in church having a great respect for pastors and their wives. We were taught not to cross them, to always be polite, and when they asked you to do something, do it with gladness. Now we are in a totally new generation of people where respect and values are almost obsolete. To execute them raises quarrels, especially when you've become too common with the congregation. We are to be a family, supporting each other, laughing together, crying together and even rejoicing with each other. But there are times when hanging out together outside of church too much breeds familiarized fellowship that, if not careful, is hard to put back into perspective. This can be very sensitive and touchy because you want the House to be in a standing that is pleasing to God. What I mean by touchy is sometimes the only shoulders you, as a leader, can cry on are those of your own fold. To go and reach out to others can be damaging when they violate the confidence. You are then put into a situation as a leader to be isolated and fervently in prayer in this place of loneliness. The flesh sometimes will rise up and make you feel as though no one understands you, your pain, or where you are trying to go. If acted upon, decisions made could bring about reproach.

Let's look at this very familiar passage of shame demonstrated by one of the Prophets.....

At the same time spake the Lord *by Isaiah the son of Amoz, saying, Go and loose the sackcloth from off thy loins, and put off thy shoe from thy foot. And he did so, walking naked and barefoot.* Isa. 20:2, KJV. After looking at this passage of scripture where God spoke to Isaiah and told him to go and loose the sackcloth from off thy loins all for a purpose, I can remember the seasons of strippings in my life. As leaders, we all will experience stripping seasons of the old wine skins in order for the new ones to come forth so that we will be able to contain the new wine when being poured into us. Let me recount the strippings for you: (1) I had to give up my position as the head of the Women's Department and couldn't do any more Women's Conferences because of sabotage; (2) The monthly marriage sessions for married women that I led were cancelled; (3) My role of Praise and Worship leader was taken away. Bookings even stopped; (4) A minister of the Gospel but sat down; and (5) Wife to the pastor but forced to give that up, too. This resulted in divorce, a decision made out of pain and suffering. I was instructed by God not to move so I had to stay right there suffering dishonor during the union and, for certain, after the divorce. Reduced to what seemed to me an empty place, I went out full but now am empty.

The nakedness of the seasons was so cruel that I prayed every day, God please move, please do something. Nevertheless, in His timing was stuck in my mind. I then had to embrace where I was for a season and say, OK, what is it that I need to learn in this?

Many leave God for this very reason, but to stay shows great love for Him. We can't be confident in positions, titles, or people as scripture says, but we must be confident in God. With all that was taken away, the love for my Father grew even stronger because I had to totally depend on Him in this desolate and unwanted place. The looks and treatment from congregants told me how they truly felt. I was stuck in a place where the strength of God was what kept me. My name around the city was....SHE IS CRAZY, FOOLISH, STUPID, and there is no way I would be there. I had to keep telling myself I have a charge to keep and a God to glorify.

God told Isaiah, put off thy shoe from thy foot. He's now barefoot. The songwriter says, got on my traveling shoes. The traveling shoes were even taken off. Think about it, you may walk around your house barefoot, or you may take off your shoes if you shout or something, but there aren't too many places you will go with no shoes on. To hear God say stand still, I was like, OK, I have no shoes on anyway Father so I can't move. He wasn't giving directions but He was giving instructions when He told me not to make any hasty decisions. *Thy Word is a lamp unto my feet, and a light unto my path.* Ps. 119:105, KJV. Walking barefoot caused me to dig into the Word and allow it to be the lamp that lights up my path. I had to become a walker and doer of what the Word says, while on a display of shame. Every step had to be that of revelation. An understanding of everything I was doing had to be first. I couldn't just do whatever because so many eyes were on me. Sure, I wanted to take a path created and produced by my own imagination, but what would I have prospered in that? He then lit up the path and said to start singing again. When I started singing again, many were looking at me as to say, Why doesn't she just sit down? But I had to keep pressing on and be obedient while embarrassed. BUT GOD !!! The human way of looking at this would have been I had every right to leave. I was not obligated to stay and subject myself to this level of humiliation. The spiritual way of looking at this was that I still must be faithful, loyal, loving, submissive, and accountable in a place where God planted me. This despite people seeing the need for me to uproot. I had to stand, because that was what God had spoken to me. If you've left your position in the House because of sabotage or disrespect, you need to find your way back. If you preach, you need to preach your way back. If you prophesy, you need to prophesy your way through. If you sing, you need to sing your way through. If shamed, you need to stand your way through the shame.

God promised double for the shame. Jesus went through shame and He is our great example of how to go through and despise not. We, too, can go through and despise not the shame to get to our set place in God where there is a promise of double for our trouble. It is our nature not to want to be shamed. But the ways of God are unknown and He chooses the foolish things of the world to confound the wise. Shame seems foolish but has a purpose that can work for your good. If you have a struggle with pride, enduring shame will strip it off for your good and clothe you with humility. Pride goes before destruction, but if we humble ourselves under the mighty hand of God, He will exalt us in due season. We cannot exalt ourselves or allow people to exalt us before time and cause a shipwreck in our ministry. Stay where the grace of God has you right now so that you may be protected. In your shame He is still building you, making you over, and equipping you farther than you can realize. Don't get caught up in the people; keep your eyes on God. He can birth in you a nevertheless spirit to say not my will but thy will be done. This is a dying process for real, and it's obtainable. If you can remember I will receive double for this, I was anointed for this, I was chosen for this by God, that in itself will give you the strength to keep on standing because your reward is on the way.

But the end of all things is at hand: be ye therefore sober, and watch unto prayer. 1 Pet. 4:7, KJV. There is an end to your shame. Just as tests in school or on your job are given, they don't last always but are for a period of time. So it is with the season of shame. The most important thing to remember in the test is to keep your mind on Him so that you can be in perfect peace. The enemy will come to try to disrupt your peace of mind, distract you with all sorts of things ranging from bills, kids, confusion in the family or on the job, and even in the sanctuary but you have to connect with that peace to be clear minded to pray. The ultimate goal of the enemy is to keep you frustrated and out of control about what is going wrong so that you pray your agitation and not the discipline of God (His Word) to bring about the needed change. Remember all staring eyes are not those of people who just want to kill your destiny; some are eyes of those who need to see somebody standing to give them hope. You never know what people on the inside or outside are facing. But for the glory of God being revealed in you, you are named of the righteous as one that is strong and can handle much, which gives them strength.

PRAYER

Father God, thank You for being the all and all in my life. Thank You for always knowing what is best and when it is best in my life. You are the orchestrator of my total being. You are the Shepherd who makes me not to want. I thank You for keeping me during the shameful seasons of my life, for in Your Word You have promised double. You are not a man that You shall lie nor the son of man to repent because Your Word assures us that we can stand on knowing that what You have promised is yes and amen and shall be made good. Thank You for seeing the best in me when I couldn't understand, upholding Your anointed with Your strong hand for it was You all along that never left nor forsook me. My heart will safely trust in You always for in You there is no failure. In Jesus' name I Pray, Amen.

5

Competition with the Church

Now there was a certain man of Ramathaimzophim, of mount Ephraim, and his name was Elkanah, the son of Jeroham, the son of Elihu, the son of Tohu, the son of Zuph, an Ephrathite: 2 And he had two wives; the name of the one was Hannah, and the name of the other Peninnah: and Peninnah had children, but Hannah had no children.

—1 Samuel 1:1-2 (KJV)

The biblical story of Elkanah, Peninnah and Hannah reminds me of current-day relationships between pastors, their churches, and their wives. Specifically, I have, and I am sure you have, too, heard a lot of married pastors say, I am married to the church. So, what this means is they have two wives — both God-ordained. This raises a lot of conflict when the church begins to assume the role of the housewife, up to and including fulfilling the duties that are only to be fulfilled by the housewife. Needless to say, this brings competition between the two. Yes, in Elkanah's day, having more than one wife was permitted, but not ordained, for the purpose of solving a problem. However, in the beginning when God created Adam and Eve, there is no account of God making another woman for Adam just in case Eve couldn't perform her duties. He told them to be fruitful and multiply. This became the benchmark for blessings and wealth. In those days, women who were barren were considered accursed. But God sometimes allows barren seasons just to show forth His glory. Hannah was barren but Elkanah needed children to distinguish himself as being wealthy and blessed. To solve his problem and keep his beloved Hannah, although he could have put her away for being barren and classified accursed, he married Peninnah to produce what Hannah couldn't at the time. We have to be careful how we word things. Clichés are not scripture-based and can put the house OF GOD in error and confusion if we try to live by them and not the word of God. Let's look at what Paul says,

For I am jealous over you with godly jealousy: for I have espoused you to one husband, that I may present you as a chaste virgin to Christ. 2 Cor. 11:2, KJV. The NIV version says, *I am jealous for you with godly jealousy. I promised you to one husband, to Christ, so that I might present you as a pure virgin to him.* Hear me now, Paul says the church was promised to Christ, not to the pastor. How can the church be presented to the true husband if it is already married? I have heard the "the pastor is married to the church" mantra for years and believed it until I was faced with the devastation that the misinterpretation of this one saying causes. In reality, the pastor has a commitment to the church and is accountable for the souls entrusted to him but he is not married to it. He is more of a marriage counselor who makes sure the church is in right standing with God and positioned to be ready to return with the bridegroom when He comes.

LATOLYA COHEN

Hannah was in a position that a lot of first ladies are in when they are in ministry with their husbands, that of a barren season. Some first ladies may come to the position equipped and some may come not knowing a thing about the position. The latter are the ones who have to be made in the position. All of us have to learn where we are and how to handle where we are; how to pray through where we are so that we may become who God says we are, where we are. You may feel neglected when many other leaders in the church are being birthed into their positions by your husband yet you seem to be left alone to figure it out. Spiritual ministries start popping up all over the place, i.e., children's ministry is being pushed and supported, Sunday school department is being pushed and supported, soup kitchen is being pushed and supported, the ministry team is being pushed and supported. But when you are crying for attention and want to move forward in your ministry and need your husband's help, he asks, what's wrong? He follows up with 'I'm not looking over you, I'm good to you. Just follow me.' Elkanah asked Hannah, who was so distraught because she was barren, am I not better to you than ten sons? Going into the mind of Hannah, I feel as though she was crying out saying, you are a great man (no intentions of tearing him down with her words) but, honey, understand the deep pain that I feel is that of a woman who wants to fulfill her duties to maximum capacity and birth forth a part of you from the depth of the love you have for me. I'm sure this goes through the minds of a lots of pastors' wives during their barren season. Peninnahs are all over the place parading and provoking you and boasting: Look, I'm doing this or I'm doing that and say, she doesn't do anything or maybe she can't do anything. Then they start saying or feeling that they are more qualified to be where you are, and commenting that you are of no use. You're sitting back watching, being taunted and picked on and having things rubbed in your face. It provokes you to pray because Elkanah is going on with ministry thinking everything is fine and not feeling the depths of your pain. The church can be very cruel especially if it covets who you are and what you have. There are some who will compete with whatever you do just to gain attention and will go as far as trying to prove they're the one and you're not. They will blackball you, sabotage everything you try to do, twist your words, and try to shut you down all because of jealousy. It's sad but true. Peninnahs will do all of this in the House of God. People bring this stuff into the house with no fear and reverence because they feel they're birthing out what you can't and they're more needed here than you are! Don't let it be a prophetic ministry, and a Peninnah comes who is birthed in the prophetic! She will flaunt her gifting and say that your husband needs a wife that's a prophetess. That you can't "see," not knowing the work that God is doing in you. The strength that God provides you to go through the suffering and pain, behind-the-scene praying to cover the ministry and the man of God, all develop you and cause you to give birth in due season to who you are and the way you need to be according to God's original design. Don't let the Peninnahs push you to bitterness. If they already have, turn the table on them and let your emotions push you to bring forth your purpose.

Looking back at my situation, I'm sitting here shaking my head at the extremes people went to in order to vex me. Just realize, as I have, this is not about you, but about the anointing being birthed in you to carry out the purpose for your life. It was not easy to get to this point. But with much encouragement to myself and from the people He surrounded me with, His grace and that alone kept and maintained my mind through it all. Why do I say this? This very situation of competition broke down barriers in my home and in the church. I was to the point of feeling like Jeremiah in his complaint, Lord, why do you have me here for these people; trying to be who you chose me to be, speaking what you tell me to speak, singing what you tell me to sing, preaching what you tell me to preach, only to be stoned and whipped, shamed and publicly ignored as though they choose to hear only from selected ones. When barriers are broken down, there is little to no protection against what now can enter into your atmosphere. If not careful, people will try to plant seeds of division in your relationship, and cause the two of you to look at each other with eyes of distrust. Cunning and crafty words will begin to operate through willing vessels to try to cause you and your husband to compete. And that is not God, nor is it good. Words such as, he is anointed to do that, not you; he is the pastor and when he speaks we respond to him not you, are uttered. When I led praise and worship, I heard it said to my husband, 'When she leads, it's hard to follow her. But when you take over, I can follow you better.' Now that the seed has been planted in your husband's ear, the divider rushes out to take over saying, 'I can do it better.' This is seen so much in churches all over. And the result. Broken down barriers allow a wedge to come between the marriage and factions of division in the church. Some will say, I will hear her and some will say, I will hear him. In all honesty, the union was created not to be handled as two but as one. Yes, the pastor is chosen, and there is only one head. However, just as the wife is the help meet in the natural, so she is in the spirit. They stand as a team unified and in agreement with the original design exemplifying the marriage that Christ has with the church. Team work is a beautiful, harmonious thing when done correctly.

During this time of competition, it was very important for me to pay attention to what God required of me rather than how man made me feel. Never operate off of the feelings that adversity brings; only divert them to strong praying and fasting so that your vexation places a demand on heaven. In turn, God grants your request and causes you to bring forth in an atmosphere where you once were counted out. God has a set time for your bringing forth, which will confuse the mind of man but will show forth His glory. Such was the case with Hannah. The same God right now was the same God back then. So much can get accomplished when everyone knows their duties. There is absolutely no need for competition in any operation of ministry; everyone has their own unique anointing that God has gifted to them.

PRAYER

Father, who is in heaven, You are awesome in all of Your ways. Your thoughts are not as mine neither are Your ways like mine. That's what makes You the all-knowing God. When my natural mind can't comprehend Your arrangements that were predestined from the beginning, You being God make it all work together to fit into Your plan and bring such insight while we, as Your workmanship, remain submitted and committed unto You. During the times of trying and proving, thank You for pushing me into a place in prayer that renders divine results in places I thought could not be. You said all things are possible unto him that believe. I will continue to trust You in the fullness of who You are because you are the God who never fails, and will continue to seek the kingdom of God and Your righteousness knowing that then and only then will all other things be added. In Jesus' name I pray, Amen.

6

Becoming A Prayer Warrior

Blessed be the Lord my strength, which teacheth my hands to war, and my fingers to fight:

—Psalms 144:1 (KJV)

Becoming a prayer warrior is a necessity for a first lady. When you can't verbalize things to anyone you can take them to the Lord in prayer, which will benefit not only you but the body of believers attached to you. When first walking into my role as a pastor's wife, I thought my husband would really hear me out on things. That people in the church would be so nice. Furthermore, who would want to harm God's elect? To my surprise, I soon learned that there is so much warfare in the lives of God's chosen. Why?, you may ask. I surmise that it is because the enemy does not want the vessels God chooses to expand the Kingdom of God to stay focused.

Leaders are a main target for the enemy. When they stay focused, people lives are changed, homes and families are restored, debts are cancelled, cancer dries up in bodies, HIV leaves, and minds and hearts are converted to totally follow Christ. And you think the enemy is not mad? The trick that he loves to pull is to send distractions to keep us from being of the same mind and the marriage in a state of uproar. It is very important to ask God to sharpen your discernment to recognize the plots and be keen on where they're coming from so you can use skills to send them where they have to go. People are not your target; that spirit that they operate in is. Evict the spirit not the person.

God teaches first ladies how to effectively target and war against the attacks launched at our ministries, marriages, families, etc. Our first reaction to the attacks is to get mad, which is OK if we let it make us mad enough to do something about it instead of sitting around and letting it reign as though it has all power. No! No! No! That only keeps us worrying about what God has given us the power over and which spiritual weapon to use to manifest the victory.

Before learning this, I would get so mad at what was going on right before my face. I just wanted it all to end, not knowing that there was a more excellent way if I humbled myself under the mighty hand of God, 1 Pet. 5:6, KJV, and He would give me a heart of compassion for His people. This was not an overnight thing, please hear me out. I first had to be delivered from some things. As long as we live, God still will be perfecting us as we die daily on this walk. You may ask yourself, What is He delivering me from?

All of us have a past. And in that past, we were trained or we learned how to defend ourselves and those whom we loved in a certain way. When you submit your ways to Christ, there must be a mind transformation. He says in His word, *For my thoughts are not your thoughts, neither are you ways my ways, saith the Lord*. Isa. 55:8, KJV. What is he saying here? Well, let's talk for a second. We believe that the way we think or feel about something is sometimes how God should feel about that thing. Our thinking on things sometimes could be far from God's perspective. When you allow Him to teach you to war, you will find the urge to pray for those who despitefully use you and persecute you, love those who purposely do you wrong, and feed those who you know are talking about you and stabbing you in the back. In other words, it is just the opposite of our carnal mind. I have witnessed so many battles won by operating effectively in prayer, by allowing Him to cleanse my heart that I may not hold up anything He needs to do, and by listening to the instructions He gives to me while I am praying. God will lead you to operate by His word. Prayer changes you and then allows God to be seen through you. Lord, change that thing.

You can never go wrong praying God's word skillfully. Why do I say skillfully? Because I am fully aware that people also use the Word of God to perform evil things against people. That's not our focus. Our focus is to cover all areas, pray against attacks launched, and pray with love. *Greater is He that is in us than he that is in the world. 1 Jn. 4:4, KJV.* There is a love that is in you that covers a multitude of sins. Praying from that standpoint helps you cover without judging, target without prejudice, and fully allow the spirit of God to use you without having to navigate through things. The most powerful thing you can do is to get on your knees. When matters push you there, seize the opportunity and just engage. Sometimes you may have to turn that plate down, ladies. Much can be accomplished in doing this. How bad do you need change? Distractions will come to try to knock you off your post because the enemy knows the damage you are getting ready to cause. Pray anyway!!! Sometimes you may be the only one praying, and that's OK, too. Agree with God, touch and agree with Him!!

PRAYER

Father God I bless you for your awesomeness. The mind of you is that of Greatness. Your thoughts and ways are higher than the human mind can conceive. Help me to embrace that it was you who chose me for this assignment. It was you O Lord, who called me forth from my mother's womb. Your word declares you are able to keep that which is committed unto you. Father I commit my all into your hands. I cast down every evil imagination that exalts itself against the knowledge of you. Imaginations of incapability to fulfill my chosen place. Peace shall be the ruler of my spirit that shall now find rest in relying totally on you. It is a Must that I stay committed to the mission and faithful to the mandate. Let thy Glory be revealed in Jesus Name I Pray... Amen

7

Receiving While Bleeding

*The Lord is near unto the brokenhearted; and
saveth such as be of a contrite sprit.*

—Psalm 34:18 KJV

While sitting here writing, a story came to mind about the pastor/wife team, Rapheal and Tracy. Rapheal grew up without a father present in his life. Because of this absence, he began to gravitate to a place that he thought would fill his void. Needless to say, that place was the hard core streets of Compton, California. The brotherhood of the gangs welcomed him as their family and began depositing into him the mindset and perspectives of a man from the streets. He quickly became a drug dealer's dealer, high ranking lieutenant, a sought out hustler. He was well-known so much so that many dealers wanted him on their blocks. Whatever he put his hands to do seemed to excel. One day the hustling life became so overbearing that Rapheal got very careless in his dealings. Now he needed some pleasure to go along with what became his busy lifestyle. How did I forget to mention that Rapheal was a ladies' man. You know, the one that everyone wants a piece of. This is the moment that you look back on your life and say, Oh, I knew one of them. OK, back to the story. Girls began to be drawn to him because of his warm personality and heart of gold that he didn't know he had, but others could see it. They wanted to be wherever he was. If there was a party going on, and they found out that he was going to be there, they knew he would be the life of the party and that this would be the party that would be live and popping. Other dealers began to pay attention to the popularity that Rapheal had with the ladies. Jealousy arose and they began to search for ways to bring him down. To no surprise, they used the very thing that caught his eyes, women. They paid women to get him off his game and off the streets. There were many failed attempts. But one day the trap that was set worked. There was a knock, knock, knock at the door of one of Rapheal's beach houses. He looked out through the peephole and saw four beautiful women with silky smooth butter brown skin, long wavy hair, flawless makeup, perfect shapes, shorts that showed the roundness of the perfect buns, and matching tops that revealed cleavage for days. He could not resist the lure of the powerful attraction that was pleasing to his eyes, so he opened the door. As they were coming in, he stood back and watched. In came the first one, then the second, next the third, and last the fourth. He wiped his eyes in disbelief, shook his head and thought, Is this really happening? Are these four beautiful women coming to see me? As soon as the fourth one came in and he was done wiping his eyes, he began to close the door, but hold up! Shots began to be fired and guys began bum-rushing the door, forcing their way in. The girls took cover as the guys now had Rapheal face down on the floor, threatening to take his life. They robbed Rapheal of everything he had, from drugs to money to clothes, and jewelry, then left. Stay with me. I'm going somewhere with this story. When Rapheal got up off the floor and looked around after they had left, he saw that not only was his stuff gone but the women were, too. They set him up to be robbed. He was filled with so much anger about what had happened that he couldn't rest that night. He paced the floor all night and called all of his friends that he could think of to tell them what had happened, each one more hyped than the other and ready to take revenge for Rapheal's sake. They began to ask questions in the streets about the robbers and someone told them who they were. Rapheal spotted them two nights later. He was suited up with four guns on him, ready to make them pay for what they had done. He began firing off, bang, bang, bang, and they were running so fast that he didn't shoot one of them. But the police heard the commotion. They came around the corner and spotted Rapheal speeding off in a hooptie and stopped him. They asked for his license and registration. He was sweating so and was still so amped up that he couldn't provide them. They proceeded to ask him to get out of the car and looked in the back seat where they saw guns under the seat. They questioned him on the shots they had just heard. Meanwhile, a witness described him to another cop and he called it in. So the dispatcher broadcasted the shooter's description. Now the cops that had stopped Rapheal realized that they had the shooter in their possession. They searched the car and found a total of four guns and took him down to the police station. He was charged with possession of four gun and landed in jail. He was tried, found guilty, and sentenced to two years in jail.

While in jail, Rapheal decided that he was going to make a change once and for all. He began to go to church and became saved. He decided once he was released that he would not return to what landed him there. The change was a permanent one that caused him to surrender his life to Christ. After his release from jail, he found a church home where his pastor nurtured him. God had delivered him from some past issues and addictions. Although he was not doing those things anymore, the spirit of the past and the attachments of the same had to be broken once and for all. His pastor dealt with him with tough love, rebuke, correction, and strategic instructions, which would walk him into his purpose and who God had called him to be. Three years later after he had been serving beside his pastor faithfully, the day came when his pastor felt led to set him aside for ministry. His response was one day he would be doing the same thing that his pastor was doing. His pastor gave him more instructions, telling him to continue to stay focused, faithful, and steadfast and watch what God will do for him. He heeded the instructions and God moved mightily in his life. He became a powerful man of God.

....*It is not good that the man should be alone:* .... Gen. 2:18, KJV. Pastor Rapheal had been pastoring now for a while and he knew he needed him a queen. The queen had to be made and designed by God to meet the specific requirements he needed of her as she would be walking into a great responsibility. He found his queen, Tracy, in another state, during a powerful service, as the eyes of the Lord glided his over to behold her beauty as she worshiped God. He loved his queen so much and the union was so designed, ordained and appointed by God that it was met with great warfare from the start. They fought and weathered the storm on a lot of things until one day all hell broke loose. The Jezebel spirit of witchcraft and familiar spirits was loosed in the ministry so strongly. The attack had the queen suffering in silence--dealing with emotional pain from confusion in the marriage, coming to worship with a smile while hurting inside, encouraging others while she herself was wounded, performing her duties as first lady and pretending that everything was OK. Leaders have to take a licking and keep on ticking for the many eyes that are watching. The power of prayer and the making of the prayer warrior became First Lady Tracy. She travailed for the ministry, the marriage, and her man. The more she prayed the more intense the warfare became. The Jezebel spirit paraded boldly, and the witchcraft had so much confusion going on in the leaders' marriage that sermons aimed at the queen now began to be preached. Lady Tracy felt all alone. She had no one she could talk to or pray with about the situation because all she kept hearing from God was cover, cover, cover. She couldn't be real with anyone in the church because then she would be accused of tearing up the ministry. She couldn't tell her family because this was a spiritual thing and they would only see it through the lens of the natural eye and then give ungodly counsel. This thing was so heavy on her that the only thing she could do was to take it to God in prayer. She watched as the spirits grouped and attached to people of like spirits. Sometimes God puts us in a place of feeling like the deck has been stacked against us, and we ourselves see no way out. She carried on with ministry while bleeding inside. Singing while bleeding. Smiling while bleeding. Dressed up on the outside and looking like a million dollars, all while bleeding on the inside. She walked with the pain of rejection, not being able to love on the husband that God blessed her with. His focus, romance, quality time, sweet words, etc., all had been shifted to another place. She came out of service after service shouting, ' Praise the Lord, saints,' and esteeming, honoring, respecting him, and being a loving wife to him even though she wasn't getting any of this in return. She shared him with the ministry and outside avenues to the point that there was nothing left for her. Lady Tracy began asking God to help her through this and to show her what she should be doing during this trying time. He taught her the art of ducking and serving. Even though you may feel that all the arrows are being shot at you, your first duty to God is to serve without emotions!!!!! Lady Tracy had a one-on-one conversation with God. She told Him, "God, we just had a nasty argument and I'm not being loved, honored or cherished as the help meet. This now has become silent frustration." Those were her words to God. He said, 'Listen to me. I will show you how to eat the meat and spit out the bones because I will be glorified in this.' God gave her peace in the midst of confusion all while still bleeding. She is bleeding from the shame, disarray, and embarrassment of her failing marriage in plain view for many to see. The more she tried reasoning with her man of God, the more her words were treated as meaningless. Now silent, she heard the Spirit of God say, 'Listen for my voice when he speaks.' The first thing the enemy wants you to do is to shut down the voice of God. ... *and how shall they hear without a preacher? and how shall they preach, except they be sent?*....Rom. 10:14-15, KJV. Anyone whom God anoints, calls, chooses, who suffers much and still is sent, has flaws and dies daily while leading. Many queens stop right there and say I just can't hear him because of the attack that I'm feeling. Just remember the attack has nothing to do with you. The enemy wants to stop the assignment of God from going forward. When you have a chosen union and all you have to do is just touch and agree to make it work, he will continue to wreak havoc in your home. He knows that if the two of you are focused and undistracted, you will tear his kingdom down. Lady Tracy heard God and began to have a listening ear for what the spirit wanted to speak to her. God began to drop nuggets of how to strategically pray from her lips, engage the tools and be used behind the scenes, all while bleeding. God is still God and will get to you what is needed for your assignment even if it has to come through the vessel that brings you so much pain. In some cases, not only will you be tempted to shut down on your husband but also on God. Many have stopped receiving instructions because they are not what they want to hear. He knows you are hurting and bleeding. He says He is near to the brokenhearted. But oftentimes we don't receive that because we run from the broken place. Hurt sometimes will cause you to want to take flight. Run and just get away from it all. But God is near, open up and let Him in. There is an ointment for the bleeding that will bring healing in the face of adversity.

I started with this story to show that what pastor Rapheal had to go through in the natural realm only set him up for the very thing he would have to face in the spirit realm. Women are drawn to flashy men, and they are drawn to the anointing. The enemy used the same tactics that worked on him in his unsaved state to take down the chosen vessel and rob him of his spiritual inheritance. *The thief cometh not, but for to steal, and to kill and to destroy: .... John10:10*, KJV. When the ministry is making an impact, the enemy is planning attacks. Pastor Rapheal knew what it looked like in his past but got caught up as he did not recognize it when it came at him in its new form in the spirit. It had come to destroy him of who God had chosen him to be from the beginning, and to reacquaint him with what he had learned to be from his seeking in his early years. Lady Tracy back in the day didn't have a problem defending herself when she got hurt, but in this arena there had to be a more excellent way. This place required a strong stance that God almighty Himself would brace and equip her for. Don't shut down from receiving, for the love of God in you is warring while you are bleeding. This is the most fought place for a first lady. If the enemy can get you to destroy what you are supposed to be receiving from, others in the ministry will begin to do what you do. Likewise, when you do the opposite and receive and encourage others to do the same, even though they may see what you are going through, it gives them hope. And when they are faced with hard trials they will be reminded of how God used you to set the tone saying, No matter how much first lady was hurting or how bad she was bleeding, I saw her still receiving God and pastor. And guess what? I can do the same. And you become a great example for many.

PRAYER

Pray this Prayer with me. Father God, you are the most high God. You are awesome in your ways and creativity. You are God that separates and call it good. In the beginning you separated the light from darkness. Thank you Lord for being the Same God yesterday, today, and forevermore. Thank you for teaching me, as being made in your image and in your likeness, how to separate what is good for me from things that hurt me. Yes there is a purpose for the pain, the crushing, and the chosen process, and even greater purpose to get the revelation while enduring. Teach me even the more to turn the tables and hear what the Spirit wants to say to me. Allowing my heart to remain open to you. Not to focus on the bleeding but the words that bring healing. Be attentive your Spirit alone and worship you the more. All things are possible to him that believes, and Lord I believe that even in this, you will make it good when it's all over... In Jesus Name I pray.. Amen

8

Walking in Forgiveness

But if ye forgive not men their trespasses, neither will your Father forgive your trespasses.

—Matt. 6:15, KJV

Lady Tracy had to learn the power of forgiveness. Trust is a choice, but forgiveness is a command. When you forgive a person, you still may struggle with the memories and wonder will it happen again? Forgiveness is the willingness to forgive. It's a matter of being willing. To be willing puts you into a state of mind to carry out or execute what you have been designed to do. Say this with me, I WAS DESIGNED TO FORGIVE. The scripture says, "But" meaning it's conditional. You never know what you may need to be forgiven of one day so please take into consideration that there is no violation. The enemy can send a person to be used by him to hold you hostage and hinder your blessings or your next place in God.

Yes, Lady Tracy felt she sacrificed her life, embraced the call to walk alone, was preached on, was victimized, and was lonely while married, all while she was positioned. Now, God was telling her to harbor nothing, only release and forgive. You may say, Are you serious? YES, I am serious. Your walk is not that of your own, which means you can't do what you feel you should do. Instead you must be open to the heart that God creates in you for this place. Many have given up right here because they feel like, Why should I forgive this man after all he has put me through? Or, why should I forgive that sister after all the pain she caused me? Or, why should I go back to that church after the way they treated me while I was there? There are so many eyes on you and God needs you to show forth His light. Will you be the one? Now, relating to Lady Tracy's situation, I can remember going through what I considered the test of time. A prophetic word was released to me saying I had to forgive. Can I get a little raw? Through infidelity (forgive), through lies (forgive), through abandonment (forgive), through neglect (forgive), through disrespect (forgive). Forgive them of all their trespasses. Does that mean you are weak? NO, it means you know how to operate in the Word of God. Does that give them a license to do it again? No, but the Word says we are to *Forgive them seventy times seven*. Matt. 18:22, KJV. Your protection is in the Word of God. In saying that, you can't go wrong applying the Word to any situation. In doing this, you will see the backing of God in every situation.

Let's talk a little further about why forgiveness is important. People who you meet in life are where they are for different reasons. Some are broken, some are empty, some are angry, some are unfulfilled, some are walled up, some are unreachable, some are wounded, some are lonely, some are battling rejection, others are unlovable, and many other things. Something has caused them to be in this place. Whether abandoned or left by the one they loved the most or forsaken by the one who raised them, something has caused these deep-seated emotions. Going back to the story about Pastor Rapheal, you will recall that he grew up having hard knocks. Along the way, he developed patterns that followed him throughout his life. Frequently, when people confront patterns, they either dare to change them or get uncomfortable with the change and revert back to their comfort zone. As a man of God, he still had to deal with the patterns he developed. Most of our men of God don't intentionally set out to hurt us. They just don't know how to change what has become a part of them. You may say, well, they are men of God and they should know better. God will not deliver you from what you are not ready to be delivered from. Some issues or patterns that they have think that they own them, causing them to continue to go round and round in a circle until God puts that urge in them to say enough is enough! I don't like the way I am, Lord. All of us have battled with something and God was just and merciful to deliver and forgive. He will do the same for them. That's why He reminds us to forgive if we want to be forgiven. Or He may remind us of a time when we needed forgiveness from something or someone.

The pattern may show up as fiscal irresponsibility, but you are very responsible in paying your bills on time. Should you put him out because he let the lights get turned off? Or the house note wasn't paid when he had the money to do so? Or you were called about the car note that he forgot to pay because he was running in so many different directions that the reminder button didn't work that day? We become a product of what we are taught. You can only get out what was placed in. A lot of wrong things that were deposited in us during childhood have followed us into adulthood. Some things we thought were right turned out to be the most destructive paths in the end. Pastors need to know that their hearts can be safely entrusted to us, and that we won't walk out at the first sign of failure. They find security knowing that the Queen can forgive a human error and still honor the anointing. Remember, we are creating our legacy and a lasting impression that many will follow.

Forgiveness sometimes sets them on the path to want to be better, because best is pushing and ushering them into their greatness. Forgiveness is the key. Don't be afraid to utilize that key; in return it will be the best key that you've ever used to launch a new beginning.

This is so POWERFUL because the enemy is expecting you to act a certain way when adversity comes, but God will show Himself through in such a way that your enemies will find peace with you. Prov. 16:7, KJV says, *When a man's ways please the Lord, he maketh even his enemies be at peace with him.*

Know that forgiveness is the way of God. If you want peace, show the way of God.

I spoke with a first lady who told me that her situation was very challenging and that she just couldn't bring herself to forgive. I told her that her next place or next big break could be predicated on whether she could let go and let God. Trying to proceed without forgiveness, if not channeled properly, will sometimes cause you to operate in bitterness. The reason I say sometimes is because first ladies have mastered covering it up. I call it the Anointing of Cover up!!! Some things we can hide for a period of time but not forever. Some things are concealed to give you time to heal. That's God. He knows that everybody is not on the same level. Some can readily forgive and others He may have to work on a little bit more. Thank God for his long-suffering with us, because we don't get it overnight. We learn obedience by the things we suffer. Heb. 5:8. KJV reads, *Though he were a Son, yet learned he obedience by the things he suffered.* If Jesus being a Son didn't get it overnight or at the snap of a finger, we, too, will suffer some things in order to learn how to obey as well.

Think about who you need to forgive and ask God to help you get past the pain and to only use the memory for a testimony. DO YOURSELF A FAVOR AND FORGIVE, in the words of Joyce Myers!!!

LATOLYA COHEN

PRAYER

Pray this pray with me. Lord I pray right now that you first forgive me of any sins that I might have committed before you, known and unknown. I pray for my enemies and bless them in the name of Jesus. I cover my thoughts of the past in the name of Jesus and the blood of Jesus. Help me not remember the past or the pain. That I might have peace and joy in my future as well in my presence. I break every generation curse of bitterness off my life and my children life in Jesus name. I thank you for delivering me from unforgiveness and I shall walk with my heart in readiness to forgive any offence against me, for this is the Will of God. I rebuke the spirit of grudge that will try to hold me hostage at any given time, from a free flowing forgiving heart. I will forever give your name the praise.. In Jesus name I pray....Amen

9

The Turnaround

Behold, the former things are come to pass, and new things do I declare: before they spring forth I tell you of them.

—Isa. 42:9 KJV

Even if it seems as though what you are experiencing will never end, I have good news for you. Brace yourself and get ready to shout! THERE COMES AN END TO ALL THINGS!!! I Pet. 4:7, KJV says, *But the end of all things is at hand: be ye therefore sober, and watch unto prayer.* It is comforting to know that He has ordained an end to your trials, tests, pains, hurts, shame, rejection, confusion, and anything else you can think of that you experienced. None was designed to break you beyond repair but to form you into the you that was thought of from the beginning before you knew your name. Brokenness is not bad, but the sound of it makes you cringe. Brokenness tears down the barriers that you hide behind so that you can get to that uniqueness that you didn't know existed.

LATOLYA COHEN

I must share this powerful testimony of what God did for our marriage. Multitudes of people didn't know, but many witnessed the turnaround. My husband and I went through a divorce after many attacks. We have a Prophetic Ministry and my husband is a Powerful Master Prophet who God uses mightily. So mightily that many lives are changed and people regain so much hope from the words God gives to him to prophecy. The ministry met the Jezebel spirit head on, witchcraft head on, warlocks head on, Word curses head on, and many other attacks, seemingly all at the same time. They were determined to destroy the marriage, the ministry, and us individually. Things got so complicated between us that we both thought getting a divorce was the best thing to do. My conversations with me went something like this: I don't have to go through this. I'm going to just walk out. I did not consult God about my decision but rather moved on my emotions. This thing was so much bigger than me. What I'm saying is I know that many of you can relate to this scenario. But keep reading. I can honestly say, I won't make that move again because even though we went through with it, I still wasn't released.

After the divorce, I was ready to move on with my life. It was amazing that God would let me do all that and not say a thing during that time. That's because He wanted to speak afterward. I was planning my next move and thought I was free. I can remember feeling like the weight of the world was sitting on my chest. I couldn't breathe and I felt so ashamed about my marriage falling apart. I went into grief but walked around and hid it with a smile, pretending that I was OK. That was the biggest trick ever. The force was so strong that it disconnected us physically but not spiritually. God spoke to me one morning while in 5 a.m. prayer and said, Stand Still and see the Salvation of the Lord. He then said do not leave the ministry, wait on me, it's going to work together for your good. I will not let you be humiliated. I burst out in tears at that and said, are you for real Father? He then repeated Himself. I thought that chapter of my life was over and the assignment was up. As many say, I thought my season was up. We were going to church still acting as though we were married, although divorced, waiting for the right time to tell the church. I would still sit in the first lady seat, caring on as though we were OK. We stilled lived together for a moment even after the divorce because nothing was thought out. We just did the most selfish thing we could think of. We did what we thought we needed to do without thinking about the affect it would have on those connected. I would literally have to ask God for strength every day to face this and every day He did just that. One day the Spirit of God came up in the House of God and my husband said, I can't keep living like this. Church, I feel lead to let you all know that my wife and I are divorced. I was standing there like a frozen porcelain doll. I wanted to crawl under the pews, or just run out of the church. The strength of God was made perfect in my weakness because I went numb and was saying JESUS, JESUS, JESUS, under my breathe. Everyone froze as if they were locked, stuck in time with their eyes right on me to see my reaction. I stood there with a smile on my face while crying silently inside saying, JESUS, JESUS, JESUS. He then turned around. On that day that brother was looking all suave and good, smelling good, and was as sharp as a tack. He fixed his eyes on me, we locked into each other, and he said, but we are all right church. Aren't we all right, Latolya? I smiled and said, all is well. Yes, we are all right. In my mind I immediately said, Oh, my God! He just announced that he is single, and this is about to be something else I will have to deal with as I didn't t know how long God was going to keep me there. Needless to say, we were divorced for a year and six months. A year and four months of our divorce had gone by and God still had not released me. I had to still pray for him, cover him, cover the ministry from a willing saint's perspective. It seemed as though my love for him intensified during my greatest pain. Many would say, I'm praying for you, or you don't have to do this, or laugh and giggle right in my face at the stand, but no one had any idea of the plan that God had in mind.

    I can remember a woman of God boldly coming up to me and saying, I just want to know for myself, either you love God for real or you are just crazy because there is no way I would still be here. You cannot explain everything that God will have you to do and it's not for you to explain. All He needs you to do is just participate in His plan and follow the instructions He gives. We don't understand that sometimes we will have to drink the bitter cup. Everything that's worth having requires a great sacrifice. I was anointed to stand. In doing so, God even said, I'm going to show you just how strong you are. I had no idea that He was going to put different situations before me and cause them not to affect me, but for me to pray through them. Listen reader, this took some dying to me for real, at a greater level now. I proceeded in doing what He needed by saying every day, nevertheless, not my will, but Thy will be done.

As I stated earlier, this stand was one year and four months long. During this time, he would preach sermons saying, tell your neighbor to let that man live, or I'm free, or Why are you still here? I would be shouting still at his messages and saying, amen, knowing he was talking about me, but saying to myself, do you hear him God? Now this is between you and Him because I'm only here because you told me not to leave. God said to me, hold your peace. I did just that. I must tell you that, during this time, I was not perfect. There were times I felt I had to say something to him. So I would wait until he called. I would encourage him and then slide in how I felt about certain things. Trust me. When God says hold your peace, please do it, because I didn't and saying something only aggravated my spirit; however, holding my peace as instructed kept me at peace.

There was a powerful revival taking place at the church the last month that I was there. A woman of God spoke to me privately saying, you have to leave. God has to shift you out in order to bring you in. I looked at her and said, OK God, I hear you. Now is the time. I went to church that night and a man of God said to me, God is getting ready to shift you. I cried and said, OK God. I hear you. The move that was ordained happened two weeks later. Everything was set in place, my lease was expiring, the kids were getting ready to go back to school. All of this was in the perfect timing of God. Well, I made the move and while doing so, cried the whole time because I was afraid of the unknown. All I had was a word that I was standing on, and that was my hope.

I moved back to Georgia and was there for a month now. Our conversations were changing. During the time of all the confusion, we were not able to communicate without disagreeing. He began to say things like, I miss you, or I miss my wife, or I miss my family. I had to let go and let God in order for this process to begin. One Sunday, he told the church that he was going to get his wife back. When he told me that, I was like, oh, yeah. I was thinking that I wanted to go on with my life now. A guy friend was kinda' smiling at me real good, too. I thought I had my groove back. God said, not so and stopped that quickly. My man of God said, you're coming home now and I'm coming to get you. I remember feeling like, now God, I have just started tiptoeing through the tulips. I was there, in Georgia, less than forty-five days. I stayed in Tallahassee in his view for one year and four months and not once did he have the urge to feel this way. I was out of his view less than forty-five days and he caught the vision. That man of God came and got his wife, and then stripped me of every hurt that I had gone through or that he had taken me through. Then he began to deposit back into the love, honor, and respect, and spoke into my life so powerfully that it caused God to restore us. We quickly remarried and got back into the will of God. And we are now in our new beginnings. We can have conversations on what we went through and laugh about the situations. The new beginnings are awesome and the love is so much greater. I thank God for all that He brought us through because I know that it was all Him. The restoration has refreshed many lives in the church and now is about to reach the masses to refresh many more marriages in the Kingdom. All the Glory belongs to God and the Best is yet to come.

God is the same God universally. If He did it for us, guess what? He will do it for you, too. All is not lost.

LATOLYA COHEN

PRAYER

Pray this prayer with me. First of all Lord there is none like you. U are so complete and perfect. I long to be in your presence. My king of king and Lord of Lord. The first and the Last, alpha and omega. I thank you for turning my life around. What the devil meant for my bad you turned it around for my good. Rom. 8:28 says all things work together for my good. You have given me double for my troubles and I bless your name. When I thought I was down, you picked me up. Lord I praise your name. The Glory in this turnaround outweighed the pressure of the test. You are and will remain the Master of turning things around. My soul is forever grateful in all you do, because of who you are. Continue to get your Glory in all things In Jesus name... Amen.

About the Author

Pastor Latolya K. Cohen is one of six children born to Mr. and Mrs. Royal in Cordele Georgia. She, at an early age, confessed Christ and received the baptism of the Holy Spirit. As a result was raised in the church.

She has been blessed with many talents including her most expressed---singing. While living in Georgia, she was provided the rare opportunity to help spearhead a music project with her former hometown ministry, New Birth Missionary Baptist Church. With this project her song, "He'll Bring You Out", was an instant hit and subsequently became the title of the cd. Additionally, she has sung with God's Anointed People (G.A.P.), an anointed community choir and has written several powerful prophetic songs.

Because of her love for worship, praising the Lord, and dedication to ministry, she does not mind giving her time, talent, and treasure. As a result of this, God has elevated her prophetic gifts as she ministers with her husband, Apostle Dr. L.E. Cohen lll; he is her mentor and constant strength in the things of God.

A wife, a mother, a daughter, a sister, a psalmist, a teacher, and a student. These are the very basic things that compose Minister Cohen's being. In addition to this, she is an entrepreneur as a licensed Cosmetologist and licensed Realtor. She is really on the move as a modern day Proverb 31 women.

www.ingramcontent.com/pod-product-compliance
Lightning Source LLC
Chambersburg PA
CBHW070106100426
42743CB00012B/2663